Are We There Yet?
ALL About the Planet Venus!

Space for Kids

Children's Aeronautics & Space Book

BABY PROFESSOR
EDUCATION KIDS

Speedy Publishing LLC

40 E. Main St. #1156

Newark, DE 19711

www.speedypublishing.com

Copyright 2016

FACTS ABOUT PLANET VENUS

Venus is the second planet from the sun next to Mercury.

There are many volcanoes found in Venus.

Venus is the second brightest object in the sky, next to moon.

Venus has an atmosphere and it is made up of carbon dioxide.

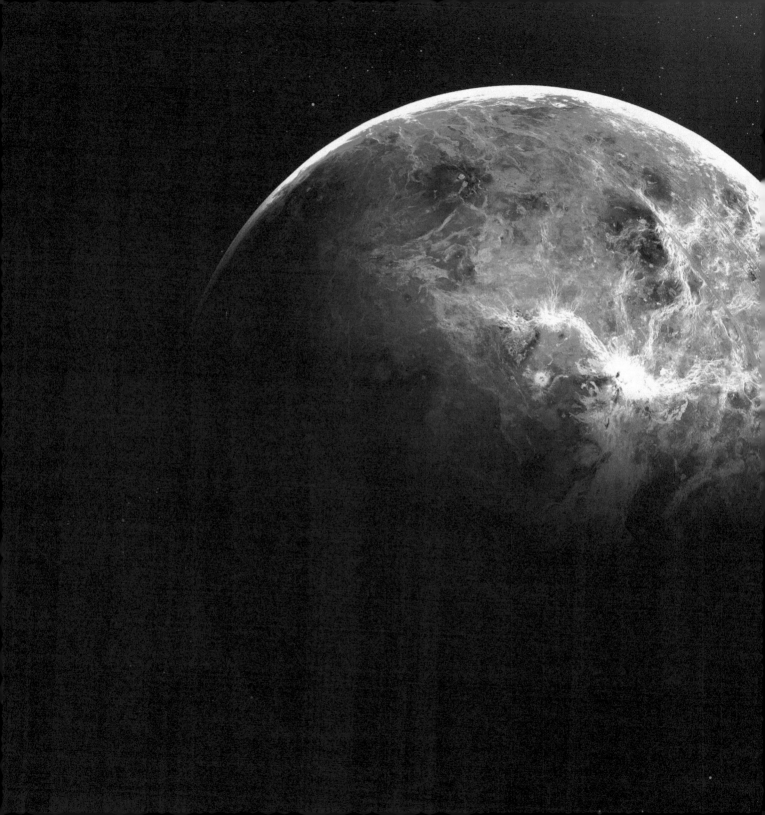

Venus is the hottest planet in the solar system.

Venus is considered as the Earth's twin because of their similarity in size and compositions.

Mercury

Venus

Mars

Saturn

Pluto

Earth

Jupiter

Neptune

Uranus

There is no
water in Venus.

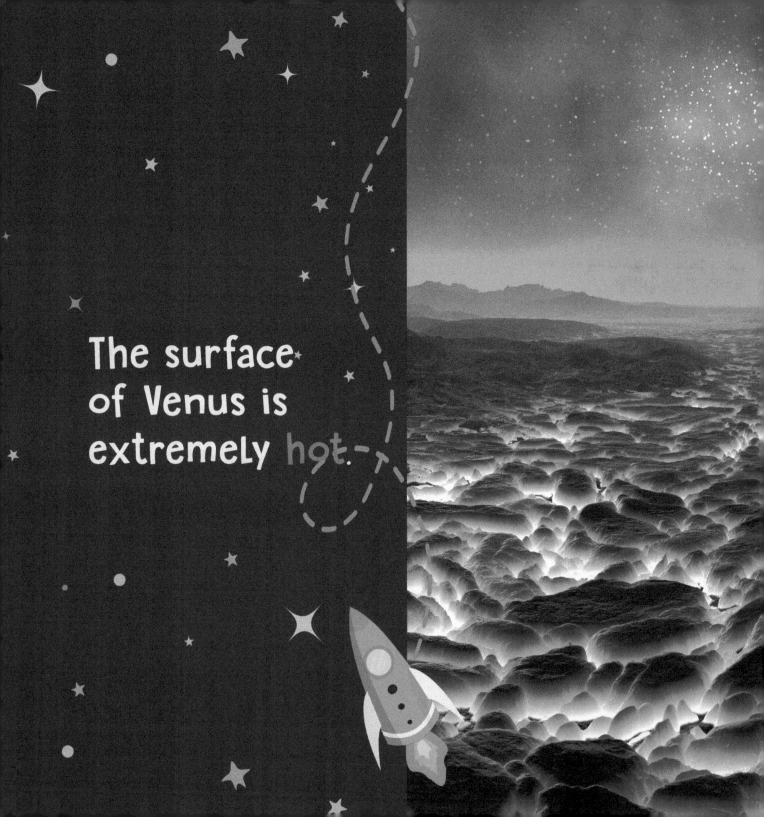

The surface of Venus is extremely hot.

Venus is the only planet in the solar sytem that rotates in the opposite direction than most other planets.

The surface of
Venus is full of
crater and very
active volcanoes.

Venus is a windy planet. It has an extreme air pressure just like the water pressure of Earth.

A day in Venus is longer than a year.

Venus has gravity similar to Earth.

The climate
of Venus was
similar to
Earth billion
years ago.

The clouds in Venus are so thick. The temperature of Venus during daytime is similar to night time.

A collision to an asteroid was believed to be the reason for Venus having a different rotation.

Venus is a bit
smaller than
its sister planet
Earth.

Did you learn a lot about Venus? Keep reading! Remember, knowledge is Power!

Mercury

Venus

Visit

BABY PROFESSOR
EDUCATION KIDS

www.BabyProfessorBooks.com

to download Free Baby Professor eBooks
and view our catalog of new and exciting
Children's Books

CPSIA information can be obtained
at www.ICGtesting.com
Printed in the USA
LVHW051550161222
735289LV00008B/1469